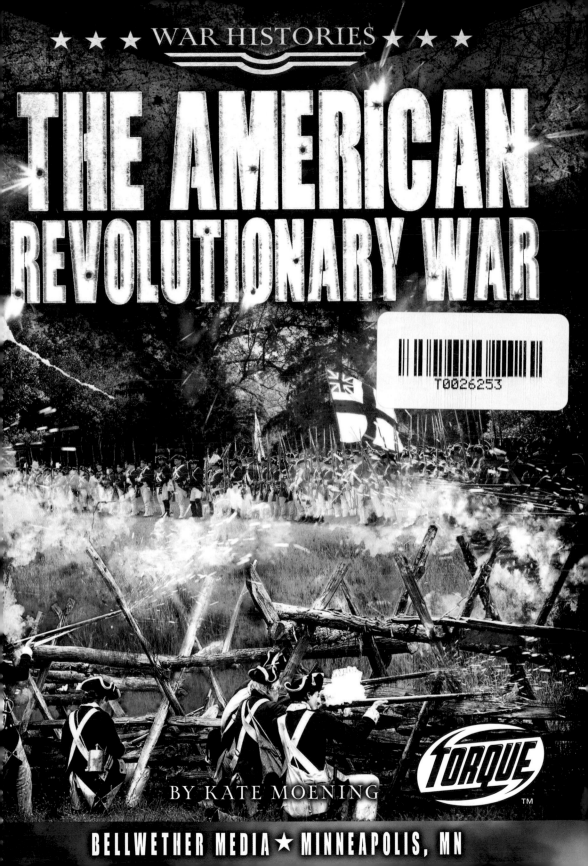

★ ★ ★ ★ WAR HISTORIES ★ ★ ★ ★

THE AMERICAN REVOLUTIONARY WAR

BY KATE MOENING

TORQUE™

BELLWETHER MEDIA ★ MINNEAPOLIS, MN

T0026253

Torque brims with excitement
perfect for thrill-seekers of all kinds.
Discover daring survival skills, explore
uncharted worlds, and marvel at mighty
engines and extreme sports. In *Torque* books,
anything can happen. Are you ready?

This edition first published in 2024 by Bellwether Media, Inc.

No part of this publication may be reproduced in whole or in part without written
permission of the publisher. For information regarding permission, write to
Bellwether Media, Inc., Attention: Permissions Department,
6012 Blue Circle Drive, Minnetonka, MN 55343.

Library of Congress Cataloging-in-Publication Data

Names: Moening, Kate, author.
Title: The American Revolutionary War / by Kate Moening.
Description: Minneapolis, MN : Bellwether Media, [2024] | Series: War
   histories | Includes bibliographical references and index. | Audience:
   Ages 7-12 | Audience: Grades 4-6 | Summary: "Engaging images accompany
   information about the American Revolutionary War. The combination of
   high-interest subject matter and light text is intended for students in
   grades 3 through 7" Provided by publisher.
Identifiers: LCCN 2023007862 (print) | LCCN 2023007863 (ebook) | ISBN
   9798886874518 (library binding) | ISBN 9798886875430 (paperback) | ISBN
   9798886876390 (ebook)
Subjects: LCSH: United States–History–Revolution, 1775-1783–Juvenile
   literature.
Classification: LCC E208 .M64 2024 (print) | LCC E208 (ebook) | DDC
   973.3/11–dc23/eng/20230221
LC record available at https://lccn.loc.gov/2023007862
LC ebook record available at https://lccn.loc.gov/2023007863

Text copyright © 2024 by Bellwether Media, Inc. TORQUE and associated logos are
trademarks and/or registered trademarks of Bellwether Media, Inc.

Editor: Elizabeth Neuenfeldt   Designer: Josh Brink

Printed in the United States of America, North Mankato, MN.

TABLE OF CONTENTS

WHAT WAS THE AMERICAN REVOLUTIONARY WAR?

★ ★ ★

The American Revolutionary War lasted from 1775 to 1783. Great Britain had 13 **colonies** in North America. But the colonists wanted freedom from British rule. They fought Britain for independence.

This war created the United States of America. It also led to **democracy** in the U.S.

THE AMERICAN REVOLUTIONARY WAR MAP

Patriots and allies

Colonies

Spain

Netherlands

France

Great Britain and allies

Britain

Hessen-Kassel (Germany)

CHOOSING SIDES

Many countries were part of the war. Soldiers from Germany fought for the British Army. France, Spain, and the Netherlands supported the colonists.

FIGHTING THE POWER

★ ★ ★ ──────────────── ★ ★ ★

In the 1760s, the British government needed money. Colonists were forced to pay new **taxes**. The colonists **protested** the taxes.

KING GEORGE III OF GREAT BRITAIN

In 1773, colonists held the Boston Tea Party.
This was their most famous protest.
They threw more than $1 million of tea into
Boston Harbor! Britain punished the colonists.
But they kept protesting.

AGAINST LONG ODDS

★ ★ ★

Britain began taking weapons from the colonists. They hoped to keep war from starting. In April 1775, British troops marched to Concord, Massachusetts. They planned to take more weapons.

HEARD 'ROUND THE WORLD

No one knows who fired the first shot at Lexington. But it became known in history as "the shot heard 'round the world."

The colonists met the British at Lexington. They began to fight. Both sides saw **casualties**. The Revolutionary War had begun. In time, the **Continental Army** was formed.

BATTLE OF LEXINGTON

Both sides fought with cannons. They also used **muskets** and rifles. But muskets often missed their targets. Troops had to get as close as possible before shooting.

In battle, two or three rows of soldiers marched shoulder to shoulder. Once they neared their target, soldiers used **bayonets**.

FIGHTING FOR THE FUTURE

Many Native American and Black soldiers fought in the war. Some sided with the colonists. Others sided with the British. Many hoped the winning side would give them more freedom.

★ THE MUSKET ★

Size:
around 5 feet
(1.5 meters) long

Weight:
about 10 pounds
(4.5 kilograms)

**Shots fired
per minute:**
3 to 4 musket balls

Accuracy:
up to about 300 feet
(91 meters) away

BAYONET

The Continental Army fought hard. But they lost many early battles. The British Army was bigger and better trained. It had more weapons.

The Continental Army had little money. It struggled to **recruit** troops. Soldiers died from disease, cold, and lack of food. Through 1775 and 1776, the British forced the **patriots** out of Boston, New York City, and northern New Jersey.

CONTINENTAL ARMY RETREATING FROM LONG ISLAND IN 1776

★ THE WAR AT HOME ★

Life was hard during the war. There were fewer goods and higher prices. Both armies sometimes stole food and supplies from people's homes.

Many men were in the army. Women took on new roles. Some ran farms and businesses. Others helped soldiers. They cooked meals and tended the soldiers' camps.

FRESH FACES

In December 1776, patriot General George Washington surprised German troops in Trenton. He captured many prisoners and weapons. His success helped recruit new soldiers.

In 1777, the patriots won the Battle of Saratoga in New York. This led France to become an **ally**. It sent troops and warships to help the patriots. France's help changed the course of the war.

BATTLE OF TRENTON

THE BATTLE OF SARATOGA
OCTOBER 7, 1777

Hudson River

Continental Army =
British Army =
fighting = 💥

A COMMON ENEMY

Many European countries wanted Britain to have less power. But they were not sure if the patriots could win. After France joined, Spain and the Netherlands also became patriot allies.

BRITISH ARMY LEADER

NAME
Sir Henry Clinton

NATIONALITY
British

RANK
Commander in Chief

IMPORTANT ACTIONS
- 1776: Helped British forces capture New York City

- 1778: Took over as leader of the British forces

- 1780: Captured Charleston, South Carolina, and most of the southern Continental Army

After France joined, Britain focused on the South. In 1780, British general Henry Clinton captured Charleston, South Carolina. He also captured nearly all of the patriots' southern army.

CONTINENTAL ARMY LEADER

NAME
George Washington

NATIONALITY
American

RANK
Commander in Chief

IMPORTANT ACTIONS

- 1776: Drove British troops from Boston in the Siege of Boston

- 1776: Surprised enemy troops in the Battle of Trenton

- 1781: Made British troops surrender at Yorktown, Virginia

People were growing tired of the war. Neither side had money. People could not afford things. There were thousands of casualties. Many people wanted the war to end.

A NEW COUNTRY

★★★ ★★★

The war's last major battle was the Battle of Yorktown in 1781. Patriot and French forces surrounded 8,000 British troops in Virginia. The British **surrendered**.

British leaders realized they could not win the war. They began working toward peace with the patriots. In 1783, American and British leaders signed the **Treaty of Paris**. The war was over. The colonists won!

★ AMERICAN REVOLUTIONARY WAR TIMELINE ★

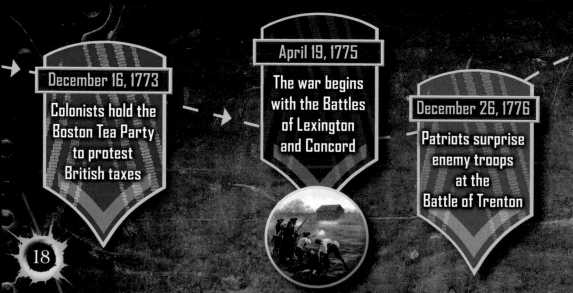

December 16, 1773
Colonists hold the Boston Tea Party to protest British taxes

April 19, 1775
The war begins with the Battles of Lexington and Concord

December 26, 1776
Patriots surprise enemy troops at the Battle of Trenton

BATTLE OF YORKTOWN

October 7, 1777

Patriots win the Battle of Saratoga

October 19, 1781

Patriots win the Battle of Yorktown

September 3, 1783

American and British leaders sign the Treaty of Paris

The U.S. became a new, democratic country. In 1788, the U.S. passed the **Constitution**. It listed the rules and rights in the U.S.

People continued to speak up for their rights. The Constitution grew. More rules and rights were added. The Constitution continues to protect rights across the U.S. today!

SIGNING OF THE U.S. CONSTITUTION

★ BY THE NUMBERS ★

1,000 Continental personnel =   1,000 British personnel =

CASUALTIES

- Around 10,623 American military casualties
- Around 24,000 British military casualties

NUMBER OF COUNTRIES INVOLVED

- 6 (Great Britain, France, Spain, Germany, The Netherlands, the 13 North American colonies)

TOTAL CONTINENTAL MILITARY PERSONNEL DEPLOYED

- 231,000 in the Continental Army

NUMBER OF BLACK SOLDIERS WHO FOUGHT

- About 5,000 in the Continental Army
- About 20,000 in the British Army

OVERALL COST FOR THE U.S.

- $101 million (about $3.4 billion today)

GLOSSARY

ally—a country that supports and helps another country in a war

bayonets—long blades attached to the end of rifles and used in close fighting

casualties—war-related deaths and injuries combined

colonies—territories owned and settled by people from another country

Constitution—the basic principles and laws of the U.S.

Continental Army—the army of the 13 colonies during the American Revolutionary War

democracy—a system of government in which people choose the leaders by voting

muskets—long guns that are loaded at the muzzle

patriots—colonists who refused to accept British rule during the American Revolutionary War

protested—showed disagreement with something at a public event with other people

recruit—to get someone's services

surrendered—gave up and decided to lose

taxes—money paid to the government

Treaty of Paris—an agreement between the American colonies and Great Britain that ended the American Revolutionary War and recognized the U.S. as an independent nation

TO LEARN MORE

AT THE LIBRARY

Gagne, Tammy. *Fact and Fiction of the American Revolution.* Minneapolis, Minn.: Abdo Publishing, 2022.

Kerry, Isaac. *The Battles of Lexington and Concord: A Day That Changed America.* North Mankato, Minn.: Capstone Press, 2023.

Silva, Sadie. *The American Revolution.* Buffalo, N.Y.: Enslow Publishing, 2023.

ON THE WEB

FACTSURFER

Factsurfer.com gives you a safe, fun way to find more information.

1. Go to www.factsurfer.com

2. Enter "American Revolutionary War" into the search box and click 🔍.

3. Select your book cover to see a list of related content.

INDEX

The images in this book are reproduced through the courtesy of: Studio 13lights, cover (Continental Army); Regine Poirier, cover (British Army left, British Army right); Domenick D'Andrea/ Wiki Commons, pp. 2-3; CBW/ Alamy, pp. 4-5; The Picture Art Collection/ Alamy, p. 6; Bettmann/ Getty Images, pp. 6-7; Fine Art/ Getty Images, pp. 8-9; Photo Researchers/ Alamy, pp. 10-11; Tower British Ordnance/ Wiki Commons, p. 11; Ivy Close Images/ Alamy, p. 12; Niday Picture Library/ Alamy, p. 13 (top); PHAS/ Getty Images, p. 13 (bottom); IanDagnall Computing/ Alamy, pp. 14-15; DEA PICTURE LIBRARY/ Getty Images, p. 16; Everett Collection, p. 17; Public Domain/ Wiki Commons, pp. 18-19 (top); National Army Museum/ Wiki Commons, p. 18 (1775 entry); United States Architect of the Capitol/ Wiki Commons, p. 19 (1777 entry); US Army Chief of Military Historians Office, p. 19 (1781 entry); Vernon Lewis Gallery/Stocktrek Images/ Alamy, pp. 20-21; Joseph Sohm, back cover.